ALASKA DINOSAURS, MAMMOTHS, AND MORE

Art by RAY TROLL   Text by KIRK JOHNSON

little bigfoot
an imprint of sasquatch books
seattle, wa

For my great grandnephews Franklin and Zachary and the next generation of Alaskan dinosaur loving kids. —RT

For Pat Druckenmiller and Jim Baichtal, our favorite Alaskan paleontologists. —KJ and RT

Printed in China by Dream Colour Printing Ltd. in August 2024

LITTLE BIGFOOT with colophon is a registered trademark of Blue Star Press, LLC

29 28 27 26 25   9 8 7 6 5 4 3 2 1

Editors: Christy Cox and Jill Saginario
Production editor: Isabella Hardie
Designer: Kerry Tremain
Production designer: Tony Ong

Library of Congress Cataloging-in-Publication Data is available.

ISBN: 978-1-63217-548-9 (Hardcover)

ISBN: 978-1-63217-549-6 (Paperback)

Sasquatch Books
1325 Fourth Avenue, Suite 1025
Seattle, WA 98101

SasquatchBooks.com

CENOZOIC

HOLOCENE — 11,700 YEARS
PLEISTOCENE — 2.6
PLIOCENE — 5.3
MIOCENE — 23
OLIGOCENE — 33.9
EOCENE — 56
PALEOCENE — 66

MILLIONS OF YEARS AGO

BIG, BIG EXTINCTION

MESOZOIC

CRETACEOUS — 145
JURASSIC — 201
TRIASSIC — 252

GIGANTIC EXTINCTION

PALEOZOIC

PERMIAN — 299
PENNSYLVANIAN — 323
MISSISSIPPIAN — 359
DEVONIAN — 419
SILURIAN — 443
ORDOVICIAN — 485
CAMBRIAN — 541

PROTEROZOIC

2.5 BILLION

ARCHEAN

EARTH FORMS 4.6 BILLION YEARS AGO

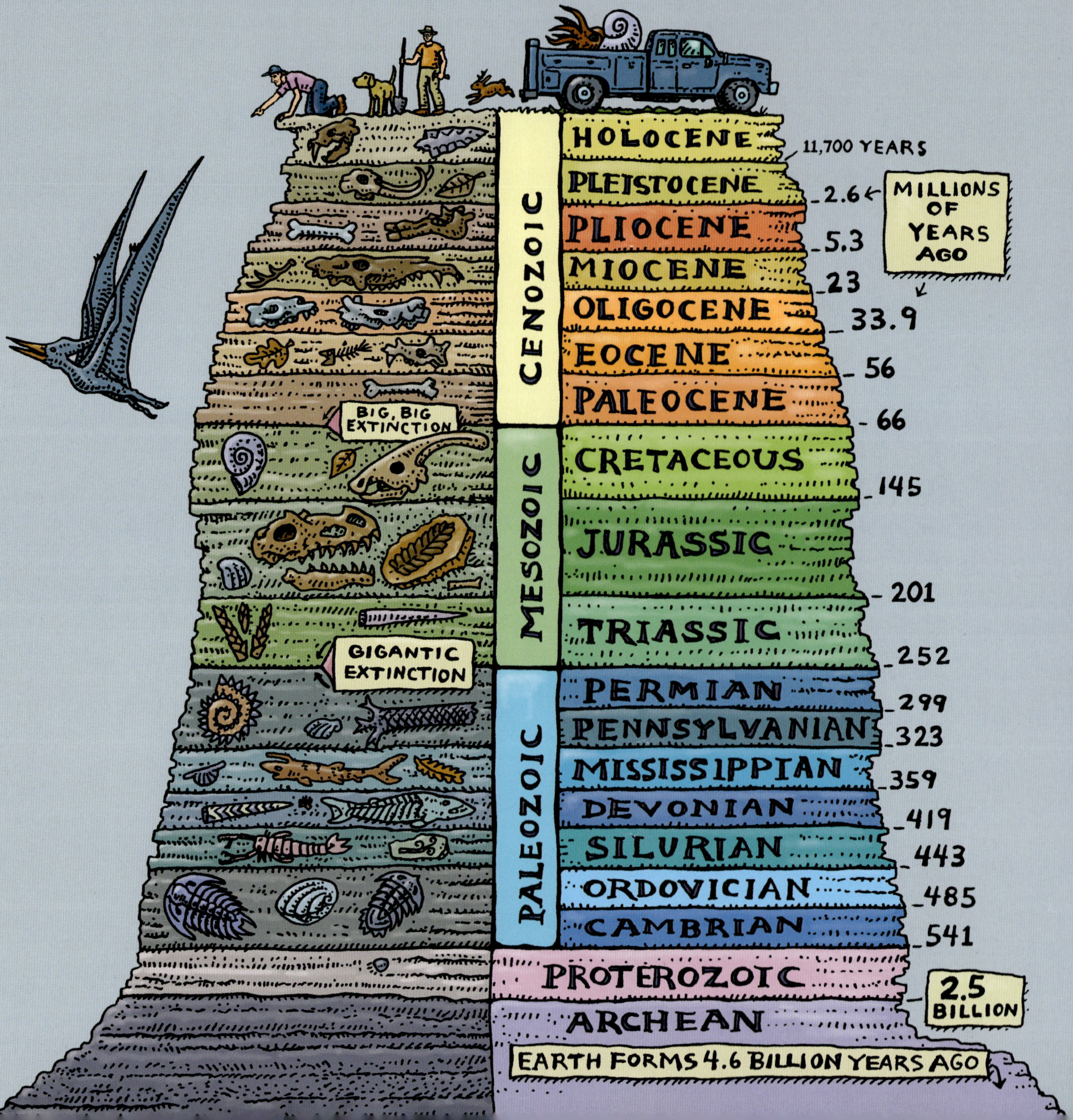

ALASKA'S FOSSILS AND ROCKS

THE EARTH is old. It has been around for 4.6 billion years. That's 4,600 million years. That is a lot of time! In all that time, rocks and fossils have stored up a story to tell. Fossils are remains of ancient life, and they are found on the ground, underground, or in bedrock on all regions on Earth, including Alaska.

Most people don't think about dinosaurs when they think about Alaska. They usually think about brown bears, moose, wolves, sea lions, orcas, and walrus. After all, it's a big, wild place! Its vast wilderness areas make fossils harder to find.

Alaska has a lot of rocks, but they are hard to get to because they are covered by forests or tundra or they are on the sides of mountains or along rocky shores. These rocks are important because they preserve prehistoric life. In places, the ground is frozen so even the dirt is as hard as rock.

Despite these challenges, paleontologists—scientists who find and study fossils—have been finding fossils all over Alaska. Other people can also find them; some important fossils have even been found by kids!

Alaska is full of people who might discover fossils while hunting, fishing, or hiking. The rocks of Alaska contain gold, copper, oil, and coal, which means that geologists—scientists who study rocks and the earth—have spent a lot of time searching for these valuable natural resources. When you are looking for one thing, you often bump into something else, and this is why geologists often find fossils.

As fossils are discovered, bit by bit, the story of Alaska's dinosaurs and other fossils is starting to be told.

Each picture on this map is based on a fossil that was found in that part of Alaska. Many of these fossils are in the University of Alaska Museum of the North in Fairbanks.

GIANT FISH LIZARD

SOME ISLANDS in southeast Alaska have rocky outcrops that were once the muddy bottom of a shallow sea. The animals that lived in that sea 215 million years ago died and sank to the seafloor where their bones were covered by mud. Over time, that mud got buried and became hard, dark rock. The rock is black and so are the fossil bones, so they are difficult to see. Enough bone pieces have been found to recognize two kinds of ichthyosaurs, which means fish lizard. One is the gigantic 50-foot-long *Shonisaurus*, and the other is the much smaller *Toretocnemus*. They looked a lot like dolphins, but dolphins are mammals, and these animals were marine reptiles.

Triassic fossils from southeast Alaska include ichthyosaurs, thalattosaurs, fish, and ammonites.

A group of hungry *Gunakadeit* searching for a meal.

NEEDLE NOSE

ONE LITTLE ISLAND in southeast Alaska has a shoreline that looks a lot like a stack of black pancakes. In one of those layers, paleontologists found the back half of a small skeleton about 10 inches long. When they got it back to the museum and slowly scraped away some rock, they realized that the body was attached to a strange-looking skull with a needle nose and sharp teeth. It was a new species of a rare prehistoric seagoing reptile called a thalattosaur! They named it *Gunakadeit* to honor the local Tlingit people's oral legends about a sea monster that brings good fortune to those who encounter it.

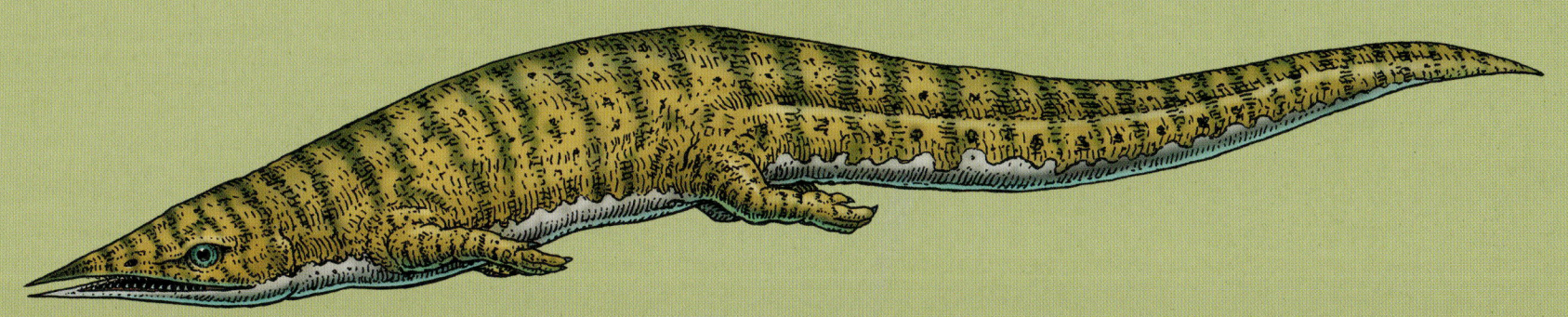

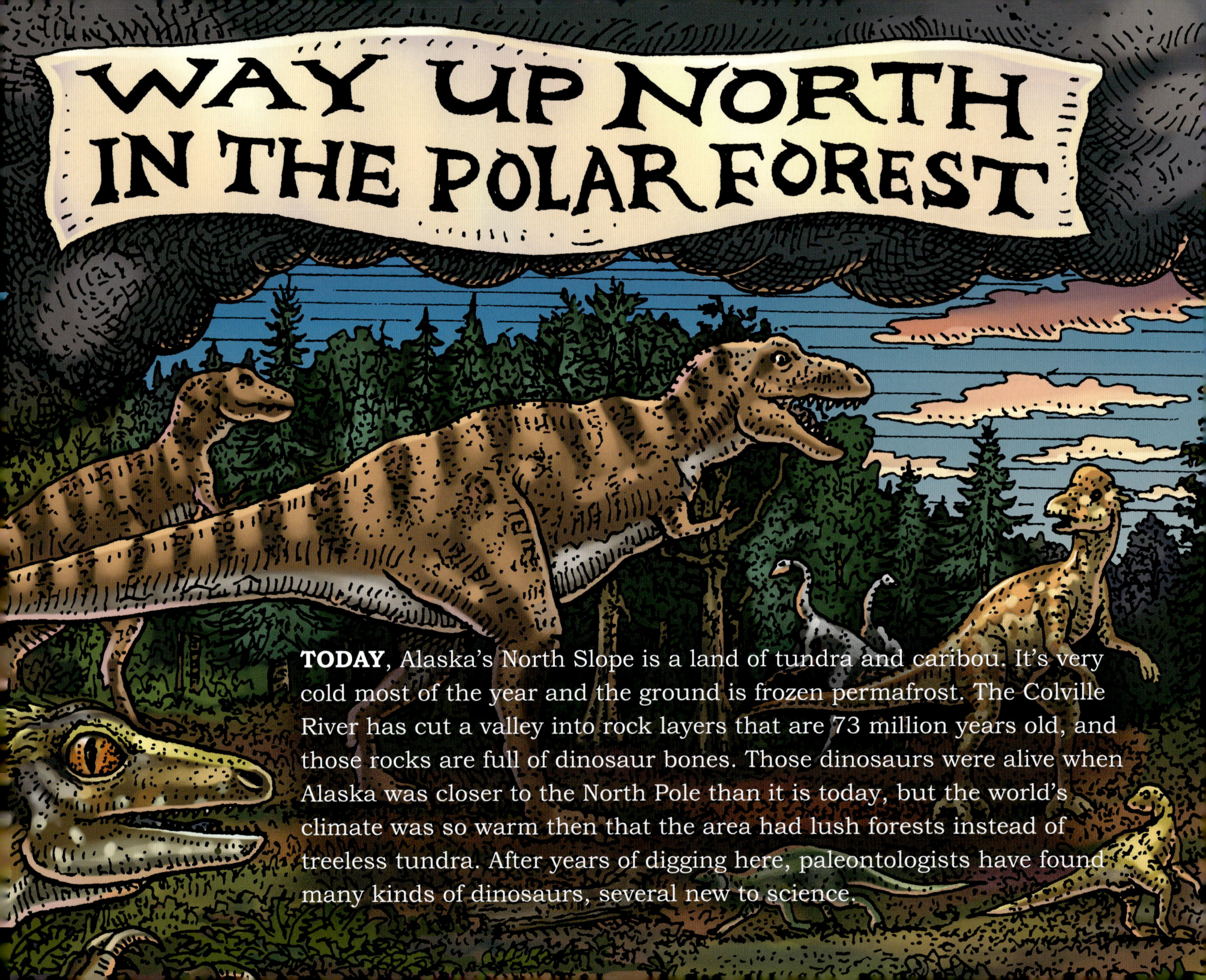

WAY UP NORTH IN THE POLAR FOREST

TODAY, Alaska's North Slope is a land of tundra and caribou. It's very cold most of the year and the ground is frozen permafrost. The Colville River has cut a valley into rock layers that are 73 million years old, and those rocks are full of dinosaur bones. Those dinosaurs were alive when Alaska was closer to the North Pole than it is today, but the world's climate was so warm then that the area had lush forests instead of treeless tundra. After years of digging here, paleontologists have found many kinds of dinosaurs, several new to science.

ANCIENT GRAZER

ALASKA'S MOST ABUNDANT dinosaur was a duck-billed plant eater named *Ugrunaaluk*. Some people call it the caribou of the Cretaceous Period because it was so common.

Along the banks of the Colville River are thick layers of mudstone packed with thousands of bones from *Ugrunaaluk* juveniles. These bone beds are evidence of events that killed and buried hundreds of young dinosaurs. There are many clues as to how this tragedy might have happened.

The bones in the bone beds are all jumbled up. Mixed in with them are the shed teeth of two meat eaters: *Nanuqsaurus* and *Troodon*. The duck-billed youngsters were probably killed by a flood and then scavenged by the carnivores. It's clear they must have been all together when they died. One idea is that these dinosaurs were living together as a herd of juveniles and were all swept away by the same flood.

A group of *Ugrunaaluk* adults guard over their juvenile offspring.

A lambeosaur in breeding colors is surrounded by smaller dinosaurs as a storm approaches.

ARCTIC HERBIVORE

THE PLANT-EATING DINOSAURS that lived in northern Alaska during the Late Cretaceous include the long-necked ornithomimids, the kangaroo-like thescelosaurs, and big duck-billed lambeosaurs. These animals survived on plants even in the long, dark winter when the sun rarely came up. It was a warm world back then, so even though it was dark, it wasn't all that cold. It's a mystery how these animals lived in polar darkness. Many animals today are nocturnal (that means that they are awake and go about their lives in the dark). If animals can be busy at night, then they might have been able to be busy for a whole winter.

Two *Alaskacephale* wandering through the forest as the sun rises in the distance.

BOWLING BALL HEAD

SOME OF THE STRANGEST of all dinosaurs, *Alaskacephale* were no bigger than a bighorn sheep and they had teeth that were as tiny as peas. They also had short blunt toenails and stubby fingers. What makes them so odd are their skulls that were almost entirely made of solid bone. Their brains fit in a small narrow chamber beneath a big round rock of a head. Some paleontologists think they butted heads with each other just like bighorn sheep do today.

KING OF THE ARCTIC!

***NANUQSAURUS* IS A MEMBER** of the same family as the notorious *Tyrannosaurus rex*. It lived about 4 million years before its bigger, better-known relative. The name means "polar bear reptile" from the Iñupiaq word *nanuq* for polar bear and the Greek word *saurus* for reptile. They reached about 30 feet in length and had large, serrated teeth, small arms, and long legs with big claws. They were fearsome meat eaters and were the dominant predators in the far north at that time. Many scientists think they had fluffy feathers when they were young. When they grew up, they didn't need the feathers to stay warm.

A BUMP ON THE NOSE

ONE OF THE GNARLIEST-looking dinosaurs from Alaska was *Pachyrhinosaurus*, which means thick-nosed reptile. This was an animal that looked like a *Triceratops* that got in a very bad accident. Instead of three big horns, this dinosaur had a bunch of small horns around its

head frill and on the back of its skull and had a big bumpy chunk of bone on top of its nose. It probably used that bony knob to defend itself from predators and to compete with rivals. Some people have thought that *Pachyrhinosaurus* had a horn like a rhino. Other people think it was just plain funny looking. What do you think?

A PACK OF TROUBLE

SOME OF THE SCARIEST dinosaurs of the North Slope were the wolf-sized raptors called *Troodon*. These guys had very big eyes all the better to see you with in the darkness. They also had razor-sharp teeth and big claws on their hands and feet. This crew of hungry *Troodon* out for an evening stroll under the northern lights looks like it's out for trouble. The skull and bones of an unlucky *Alaskocephale* show that it wasn't exactly safe to go out in the long nights of the Late Cretaceous Period of Alaska.

A pack of feathered *Troodon* out hunting in the long polar night.

SHELLS BIG AS TIRES

ALASKA HAS ALWAYS been near the ocean, and many parts of it have been under the sea, so it's common to find fossils of animals that lived in salt water. Just north of Anchorage, there are layers of shale that were once the bottom of a 70-million-year-old sea. Many fossils in these rocks are ammonites, the extinct relatives of octopus and squid. They lived in spiral-shaped shells that grew larger as the animal grew larger. Some grew to the size of truck tires!

Most ammonites had beautiful spiral-shaped shells, but some looked more like giant paper clips. They went extinct along with the big dinosaurs 66 million years ago.

Numerous trackways are perfectly preserved in the fossilized forest floors of this long-vanished world. Some are from giant birds and others from tiny four-toed horses not much bigger than a cat.

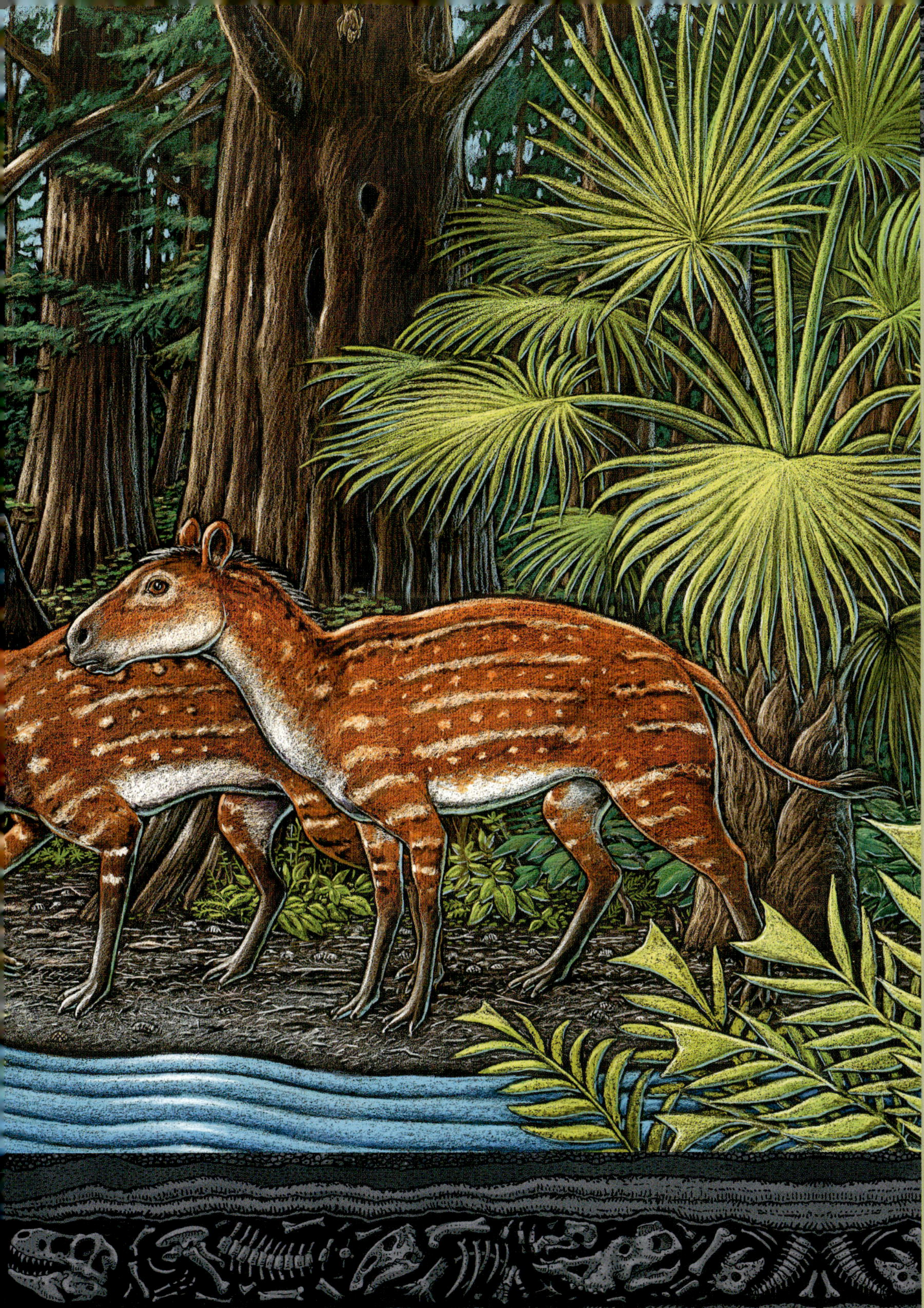

EOCENE EPOCH — 56 MILLION YEARS AGO

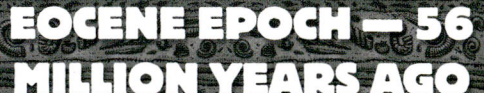

ALASKAN PALM TREES

FIFTY-SIX MILLION years ago, the coast of southeast Alaska was covered in a warm, wet rainforest that looked more like Costa Rica than Juneau. Instead of giant Sitka spruce, this forest had a mixture of palm trees, ferns, and big trees with broad leaves. Some of the animals that lived in this ancient forest were large flightless birds with massive skulls and tiny four-toed horses that were only two feet tall. The whole world was a much warmer place and had no polar ice caps. Still, the fact that there were palm trees in Alaska seems pretty weird!

PACIFIC DESMO

ABOUT 20 MILLION years ago, the coast of Alaska hosted an unusual and now long-gone marine mammal called a desmostylian, or "desmo" for short. Desmos lived in the north Pacific and ranged from California to Alaska and all the way over to Japan. They looked like hippopotamuses, but they might be related to horses and rhinoceroses. Think of them as sea horses with tusks! The Alaskan species was found in the town of Unalaska in the Aleutian Islands and was named *Ounalashkastylus*, meaning "near the peninsula" in the language of the Unangan people.

BISON, HORSE, MAMMOTH

PACIFIC DESMO

ABOUT 20 MILLION years ago, the coast of Alaska hosted an unusual and now long-gone marine mammal called a desmostylian, or "desmo" for short. Desmos lived in the north Pacific and ranged from California to Alaska and all the way over to Japan. They looked like hippopotamuses, but they might be related to horses and rhinoceroses. Think of them as sea horses with tusks! The Alaskan species was found in the town of Unalaska in the Aleutian Islands and was named *Ounalashkastylus*, meaning "near the peninsula" in the language of the Unangan people.

BISON, HORSE, MAMMOTH

THIRTY-FIVE THOUSAND years ago, central and northern Alaska was drier than it is today. Instead of tundra, there were vast grasslands. The most common animals in these grasslands were bison, horses, and woolly mammoths. The Pleistocene was a much colder world than today, which is why it is often called the ice age. This rich landscape also supported cave lions, giant musk oxen, ground sloths, Saiga antelope, and short-faced bears.

WALRUS AND POLAR BEAR

WALRUS ARE ONE of Alaska's most beloved animals. They live mainly in the Bering and Chukchi seas. An adult male walrus can weigh as much as 2 tons and be 12 feet long! Walrus spend a lot of time near sea ice. They feed on the seafloor by shooting water out of their mouths to dig clams. Between feeding dives, walrus rest on little floating ice islands. Polar bears also spend a lot of time on sea ice hunting for seals at their breathing holes. Sometimes a hungry polar bear will try to eat a walrus, but they're rarely successful since walrus are much bigger than polar bears and their skin is thick and super tough.

Unfortunately for these animals, sea ice in the Arctic has been melting, and this is bad news for walrus and polar bears because they are ice animals. These animals are ancient survivors from Alaska's prehistoric past. Their fossils have been found in Alaska and they are still alive today.